CONTENTS

INTRODUCTION

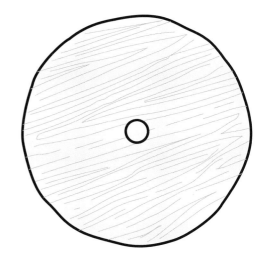

How many different ways can you think of to travel from one place to another? Buses, cars, bicycles, trains, ships and planes are all forms of transport and they all involve technology. Modern technology has even made it possible to travel into space.

The purpose of any form of transport is to move people or goods from one place to another. In this book we shall look at some of the most important and some of the most recent developments in transport technology. First, however, we shall look at possibly the most important technological development of all – the wheel.

As old as the wheel

Before the wheel was invented about 5000 years ago, people moved around by boat, or they walked or rode animals. It was very difficult to carry heavy loads even short distances. Wooden rollers (perhaps tree trunks) were probably the first type of wheels used to pull large, heavy objects. Some of the earliest wheeled vehicles may have been war chariots, in ancient Mesopotamia (now Iraq). Gradually the wheel spread to other parts of Asia, Africa and Europe.

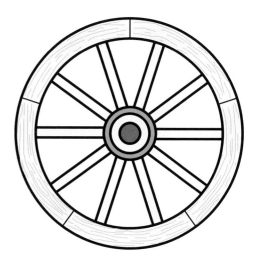

The first wheels were made of solid wooden planks. Spoked wheels were developed about 4000 years ago. They were lighter, but still strong. Wheels did not change much until about 100 years ago, when they were fitted with air-filled tyres, just in time for the motor car!

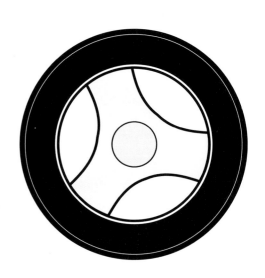

Transport

Julian Rowe

First published in Great Britain by Heinemann Library
Halley Court, Jordan Hill, Oxford OX2 8EJ
a division of Reed Educational and Professional Publishing Ltd

OXFORD FLORENCE PRAGUE MADRID ATHENS
MELBOURNE AUCKLAND KUALA LUMPUR SINGAPORE TOKYO
IBADAN NAIROBI KAMPALA JOHANNESBURG GABORONE
PORTSMOUTH NH CHICAGO MEXICO CITY SAO PAULO

Designed by **AMR**
Illustrations by Art Construction
Originated in the UK by Dot Gradations Ltd, Wickford
Printed in the UK by Jarrold Printing Ltd, Thetford

01 00 99 98 97
10 9 8 7 6 5 4 3 2 1

ISBN 0 431 06445 8
This title is also available in a hardback library edition (ISBN 0 431 06444 X).

British Library Cataloguing in Publication Data
Rowe, Julian
        Transport. - (Making science work)
        1. Transportation - Juvenile literature
        I. Title
        388

Acknowledgements
The Publishers would like to thank the following for permission to reproduce
photographs.

Trevor Clifford: p.5 (top); Action-Plus: p.5 (bottom); Mary Evans Picture Library: p.6
(bottom), p.21 (top); Associated Press/Topham: p.8; French Railways Limited: p.9 (top);
Topham Picturepoint: p.9 (bottom); Tony Stone Images: p.10; Frank Spooner Pictures:
p.12; Images Colour Library: p.13; Paul Amos Photography: p.14; Hong Kong Tourist
Office: p.15 (top); Zefa: p.15 (bottom); Adrian Meredith Aviation Library: p.18; Tony Stone
Images: p.20; Peter Russell/The Military Picture Library: p.21 (bottom); Science Photo
Library: p.24, p.25; Next Destination Ltd: p.27; Britstock-IFA: p.28

Cover photograph reproduced with the permission of Alex Bartel/The Science Photo
Library.

Our thanks to Jim Drake for his comments in the preparation of this book.

Every effort has been made to contact copyright holders of any material reproduced in
this book. Any omissions will be rectified in subsequent printings if notice is given to the
publisher.

Bridges and tunnels make journeys shorter and safer. This modern bridge is near Seville in Spain.

Engines

Using wheels, you can pull heavier loads and travel faster with less effort than it would take by hand or by foot. For thousands of years, wheeled vehicles were pulled by animals until, less than 200 years ago, steam engines were used to power trains and ships.

Steam engines were difficult to use on the road. The invention of the **internal combustion engine** led to the development of cars and then planes. Internal combustion engines are not very efficient. They change only 10–20 per cent of the energy in fuel into movement. Jet engines are reliable and produce more power.

Transport technology involves much more than wheels, engines and the vehicles themselves. Roads, railways, bridges and tunnels are all designed and built by engineers using different kinds of materials. And, unless you can navigate by the sun and stars, you use technology to find your way. This book shows how engineers are making travel faster, safer and more efficient.

Bicycles are one of the most efficient forms of personal transport. They became popular about 100 years ago, around the same time as the car was invented.

CARS, CARS, CARS

Henry Ford made the first car that was cheap to buy. Many people could then afford to go where they liked, when they liked. Today's engineers are tackling the problems brought about by the millions of cars now speeding along our roads and polluting our streets. What are engineers doing to make cars safer and cleaner?

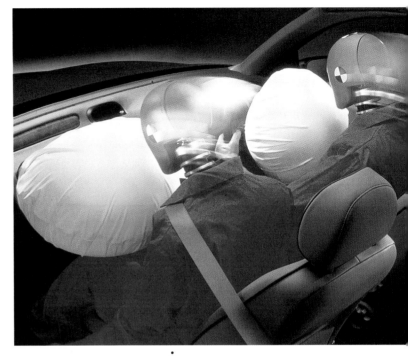

Safety

Everyone hopes that their car will never be in an accident, but designers have to prepare for the worst. Safety belts, airbags and roll bars have helped to make driving safer.

Designers and engineers deliberately crash cars! They put dummies inside cars to see what would happen to people in different kinds of crashes.

Leaner and cleaner

Most cars are still powered by internal combustion engines, just as the first cars were 100 years ago. The engines in older cars waste over three-quarters of the energy in petrol, and their exhaust fumes contain harmful gases. Many of today's cars use fuel injection. A computer under the dashboard calculates exactly how much fuel and air should be pumped into the engine so that the fuel burns more cleanly. In modern cars exhaust fumes are passed through catalytic converters. They change the harmful gases into carbon dioxide, nitrogen and water.

In the USA in 1908, Henry Ford began to produce the Model T Ford. By 1927 he had sold over 15 million 'Tin Lizzies', as they were called.

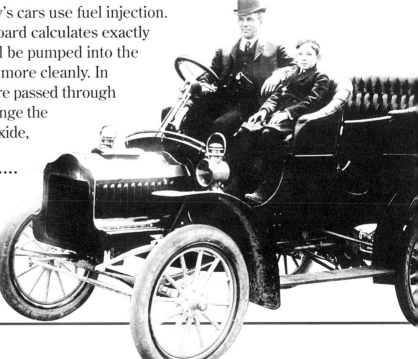

HOW AN INTERNAL COMBUSTION ENGINE WORKS

1 A small amount of fuel and air is sucked into the cylinder.

2 The piston moves up and squeezes the gases.

3 The fuel explodes forcing the piston down.

4 Exhaust gases are pushed out.

A petrol engine can have several cylinders, each with a piston. As the piston moves up, the fuel explodes and forces the piston down. As the pistons move up and down they produce the movement which turns the wheels.

Cars of the future

Tomorrow's cars will be 'intelligent'. They will drive themselves on motorways and help the driver to park. Road signs will beam information into the car about traffic jams on the roads ahead. A head-up display shown in front of the driver will show the car's speed, fuel level and the best route to follow to avoid traffic jams. The technology for all these developments has already been tried and tested.

The car of the future will use technology to make driving safer and cleaner. It will use satellites and computers to help it find the best route through the traffic.

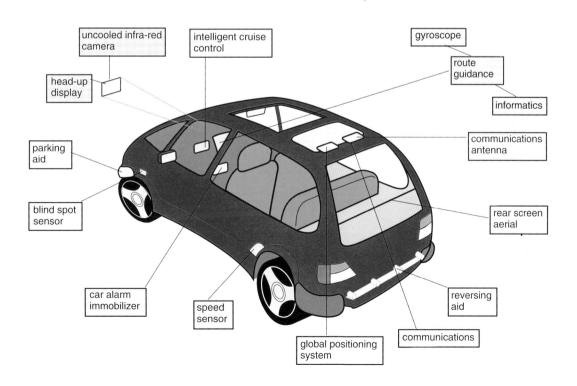

uncooled infra-red camera

intelligent cruise control

gyroscope

route guidance

informatics

head-up display

parking aid

communications antenna

blind spot sensor

rear screen aerial

car alarm immobilizer

speed sensor

global positioning system

communications

reversing aid

HIGH-SPEED TRAINS

Until the first railways were invented, most people never travelled far from where they lived. The railways made travel fast and cheap. They were followed by even faster aeroplanes, but air travel often involves long waits at airports miles from the centre of cities. Many people now believe that we are at the start of a new age of rail. Fast trains use less fuel than cars or trucks, cause less pollution and can carry a lot more goods and people. Trains travel between major cities in one country in almost the same time as it takes by aeroplane. How do they do this?

Fast trains

The fastest trains in the world are all **streamlined** and powered by electricity. The electric locomotive does not have to carry its fuel with it, but picks up electric current from an overhead wire or a third rail on the track.

Eurostar

Sleek *Eurostar* passenger trains link Paris, Brussels and London. They take just 21 minutes to pass through the Channel Tunnel, 130 metres below sea level. *Eurostar* takes only three hours to travel from the centre of London to the centre of Paris. Loops of wire along the *Eurostar* track communicate with electronic equipment on board each train. This system controls the train's speed as it approaches a station and it passes signalling information directly into the driver's cab.

Each *Eurostar* train has a specially designed streamlined locomotive, followed by 18 coaches. It is 400 metres long and travels at 200 kilometres per hour (120 mph). Cars and lorries are carried on special **rolling stock** on a tunnel service.

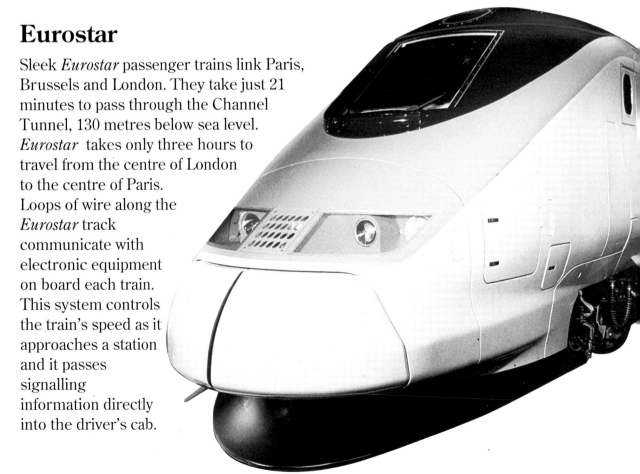

Bullet train

The Bullet train was the first high-speed train to run on special tracks. The service began in 1964 and the trains make the 338-kilometre (203-mile) journey from Tokyo to Nagoya in Japan at over 200 kilometres per hour (120 mph).

The Japanese and Germans are both developing a new kind of train which will travel faster than either the TGV or the Bullet. A maglev (short for magnetic levitation) train does not have wheels. It glides above or below the track (see page 28).

TGV

The French TGV (*Train à Grande Vitesse*) is one of the world's fastest trains. It travels at 300 kilometres per hour (180 mph). A powerful electric locomotive at each end drives the train along. It has eight streamlined passenger cars.

The Bullet train speeds through Japan on special tracks.

A *TGV* train rushes through the French countryside.

OVER AND UNDER

Bridges and tunnels can make journeys safer and shorter. The longest road tunnel in the world is the St. Gotthard Tunnel in Switzerland. It is 16 kilometres (10 miles) long and saves motorists from having to drive 2000 metres up into the mountains to cross the Alps. The extraordinary Sheto Ohashi Bridge in Japan is really six bridges in one. It links the islands of Honshu and Shilolo across the 13-kilometre-wide (8 miles) Strait of Seto. How do engineers build such huge and impressive structures?

The roadway of this suspension bridge in Houston, Texas, is suspended from long steel cables attached to tall towers near each end of the bridge. Each cable is made up of thousands of tightly bound steel wires.

Two inventions

Modern bridges, such as the Houston Bridge in Texas and the River Humber Bridge in England, would not be possible without two nineteenth-century inventions: cheap mass-produced steel and Portland cement, from which concrete is made. Hollow concrete pylons support bridges, which are then hung from strong steel cables.

SUPERBRIDGES

Suspension bridges are the longest bridges because they use the most lightweight construction. The Golden Gate Bridge spans the entrance to San Francisco Bay, USA. When it was opened in 1937, it was longer (1280 metres) and taller (227.4 metres) than any previous bridge.

Now another suspension bridge, the River Humber Bridge in England, holds the record (1410 metres), but not for long. The Great Belt East Bridge, which is now being built in Denmark, will be even longer. There are plans all over the world to build more superbridges.

One part in a million

The railway tunnel under the English Channel is 31 kilometres long (18.5 miles). Work on it began in 1987, when tunnellers started excavating on both the English and French coasts. Two years later, the tunnellers met under the sea, 21 kilometres (12.5 miles) from the English coast. The tunnels joined together exactly, within centimetres. How did the tunnellers achieve such accuracy?

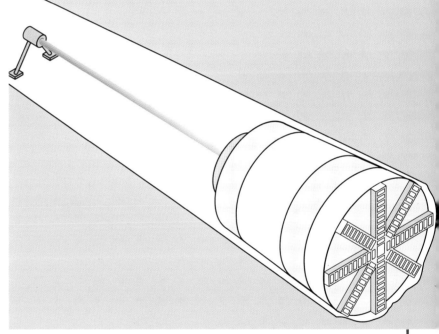

First, the tunnel entrances were lined up very accurately, to within one millimetre per kilometre (one part in a million). The GPS, or Global Positioning System, was used to do this. Next, a pencil-thin laser beam was used to control the precise direction of the TBMs (tunnel-boring machines). These giant machines, which have a crew of 50 workers, grind forwards at about 1 kilometre (0.6 miles) a month.

A computer-controlled 'target', which is sensitive to light, is fixed to the back of a tunnel-boring machine (TBM). It detects the laser beam. Information from the target is fed into the TBM's computer. It allows tiny corrections to be made to the tunneller's position.

DELIVERING THE GOODS

The largest ships afloat today are the oil tankers that carry crude oil from oilfields to refineries. In fact most heavy cargo travels by sea. On the road, big trucks transport everything from fuel, oil, wine, bricks and cars to fruit. Why is it that these giants of the sea and road are so efficient?

Tankers

Tankers may weigh up to 500,000 tonnes and be 300 metres long. Their rounded bow helps them move faster and more smoothly. Amazingly, these huge tankers are pushed through the water by a single propeller, driven by a steam turbine. (A turbine is like a propeller with many blades.) The propeller sucks in water from ahead and pushes it backwards, making the ship move forward. Most ships are powered by steam or diesel engines. Marine diesel engines produce 15 000 **hp** (horsepower) and use less fuel than steam engines.

Boxed in

Much of the world's cargo travels in 'containers' – strong, weather-tight rectangular boxes. Containers are very efficient because they are all the same size – 2.44 metres high and wide, and 6.06 or 12.19 metres long – which means they are easy to stack and to load. Containers are carried to and from the docks on railway wagons or lorries. They are lifted on and off container ships by transporter cranes. Large container ports, such as Singapore, use computers to control the arrival and departure of ships and containers.

This tanker carries oil by sea to refineries.

Delivered by lorry

The bigger a lorry the more it can carry. Long-distance juggernauts usually have an angled panel above the cab to make them more **streamlined**. The panel deflects air smoothly over the body and so helps to reduce the amount of fuel the lorry uses. Big, heavy lorries are not difficult to drive. The steering is power assisted – when the driver turns the steering wheel, the road wheels swivel easily. The system is operated by a **hydraulic** pump driven by the lorry's engine.

Trucks have many wheels to carry their immense loads. Some trailers have up to 18 wheels. The tyres are reinforced with steel hoops to make them stronger.

TURBO LORRIES

Some lorries are fitted with turbochargers to make their engines more powerful. Exhaust gases from the engine drive a small gas turbine, which in turn drives the turbocharger. A turbocharger compresses the air that the engine uses to burn its fuel. This increases the efficiency of the engine. It works with sports cars, too!

FAST FERRIES

Traditional ships move fairly slowly because the resistance of the water (the drag) pulls them back. Hydrofoils and hovercraft overcome drag by riding above the water. High-speed ferries try to compete by giving their passengers a fast, smooth ride and loading and unloading quickly. How do hydrofoils and hovercraft work and how have ferries made sailing faster and smoother?

No tugs needed

Car ferries with huge, watertight doors at either end are called ro-ro ferries (roll-on roll-off). Cars and trucks drive directly on and off the ship. Despite their huge size, ro-ro ferries enter and leave ports without the help of tugboats.

As well as having powerful engines to move quickly through the water, ferries are also fitted with bow thruster units. These consist of a reversible propeller in an underwater tunnel which stretches across the ferry near the bows. The propeller forces water to either side, allowing the ship to turn quickly in the docks.

This ro-ro ferry sails between Portsmouth in Britain and Bilbao in Spain. Some ro-ros are nearly 200 metres long. They can carry more than 1000 passengers and 800 cars.

'Pass the sick bag!'

This request is not heard much any more. This is because ferries, like many passenger ships, are fitted with stabilizers, which are movable, horizontal fins attached to the ship's hull. They are controlled by gyroscopes and automatically change their angle to prevent the ship from rolling.

This hydrofoil can travel at speed because propellers lift it above the water and prevent water resistance slowing the vessel down.

Large passenger hovercraft can carry over 400 passengers and 60 cars. Four jet engines drive the fans and propellers that form a cushion of air for the hovercraft to ride on.

UNDER THE SEA

Large military submarines patrol the world, hundreds of metres below the surface of the sea. They even sail under the thick ice that covers the North Pole. These amazing ships can produce their own oxygen and can stay submerged for as long as there is enough food for the crew. A **nuclear reactor** can fuel the electric motors for many years without the submarine having to surface. Smaller submersibles can dive even deeper. They work on underwater pipelines or explore the dark chasms of the ocean bed. How do submarines and submersibles dive and how do they find their way under the sea?

Sinking and steering

A submarine has large ballast tanks on either side of the hull. When the tanks fill with water, the submarine sinks lower and lower. To return to the surface, the crew blow the water out of the tanks using compressed air and the submarine floats upwards. When air is compressed it takes up only a small amount of space. When it is released, a small amount will expand to fill the ballast tanks.

Submarines are equipped with fin-like hydrovanes at the front and back to tilt the ship up or down. As on a surface ship, a rudder steers the ship.

This diagram shows how submarine ballast tanks work. In the picture on the left, the submarine has surfaced, by letting water out of the tanks to make the vessel light. When the submarine dives (middle), water is let in to the tanks to make the vessel heavy, so it sinks.

surfaced

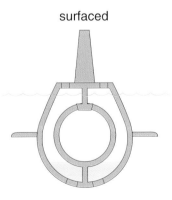

diving

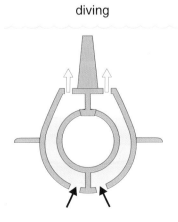

surfacing again

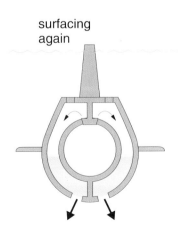

Sonar

Submarines use sound to help them find their way. Surface vessels searching for submarines under water also use sonar (SOund NAvigation and Ranging system). The sonar system sends out a sound signal and listens for the echo caused when the signal strikes the surface of a ship, or even a shoal of fish. The echo produces a picture of the object on a screen. The distance between the submarine and the object can be calculated from the speed of the echo.

Submersibles

Submersibles are small, specialist submarines that are carried out to sea by a ship. They are used for many kinds of underwater jobs, such as repairing cables, servicing oil rigs and mapping the ocean floor. They have powerful lights to help the crew see in the darkness of the ocean depths. One submersible, *Alvin*, searched for and found the *Titanic*, which sank in 1912 after hitting an iceberg.

Up periscope

When a submarine hides just under the surface of the water, with its conning tower submerged, its crew can still see other ships on the surface. They look through the submarine's periscope – a device made of mirrors and lenses that sticks up above the water. The periscope can be rotated to scan the entire horizon. Video cameras also scan above and below the surface.

SPEED OF SOUND

Sound travels through air at 331 metres per second (about one mile every five seconds). It travels through water nearly five times as fast as through air.

Submarines, such as the *USS Ohio*, are powered by diesel engines when sailing on the surface of the water. A diesel engine needs air to burn the fuel. The air is sucked in through a snorkel tube in the conning tower.

FLYING HIGH

The fastest way for most of us to travel is by aeroplane. Airliners can carry up to 400 passengers at a time and speed them from place to place at 1000 kilometres per hour (600 mph). *Concorde* travels even faster. It can carry 139 passengers from Paris to New York in just 3.5 hours. Many people are frightened of flying, yet it is the safest form of transport. How have engineers made flying so safe, and why can *Concorde* fly so fast?

Fastest passenger plane

Concorde is the fastest airliner in the world. It flies supersonically at 2300 kilometres per hour (1380 mph), nearly twice as fast as the speed of sound. It can fly this fast because it has extra powerful engines and its swept-back wings and long, thin body make it more **streamlined** than other aeroplanes.

Autopilot

Air travel is very safe because the aircraft is controlled mainly by computer. The aircraft's route is planned by air traffic control. The pilot inputs the direction, speed and height to the aircraft's computer and, once the wheels have left the runway, switches over to autopilot. From then on the aeroplane's computer controls the aircraft. The pilots watch the instruments and can always take over from the autopilot in an emergency.

Concorde's long, smooth, thin shape makes it easy to cut through the air without **friction**.

Supersonic heat

The air friction caused by flying at supersonic speeds creates immense heat. *Concorde* is built from titanium, which is an expensive metal but is more resistant to heat than the aluminium **alloys** used in slower aircraft.

WHAT MAKES AN AIRCRAFT FLY?

How does a 300-tonne aircraft become a graceful flying machine? The answer lies in the shape of its wings.

As a wing cuts through the air, air is forced over the upper and lower surfaces of the wing. While the underside of the wing is nearly flat, the upper side is highly curved. This means that air has to travel farther over the top of the wing than underneath it; this 'stretches' the air, making it less dense. As a result, the air pressure is higher under the wing than above it. The air under the wing 'pushes up' to provide the lift that keeps the aircraft in the air.

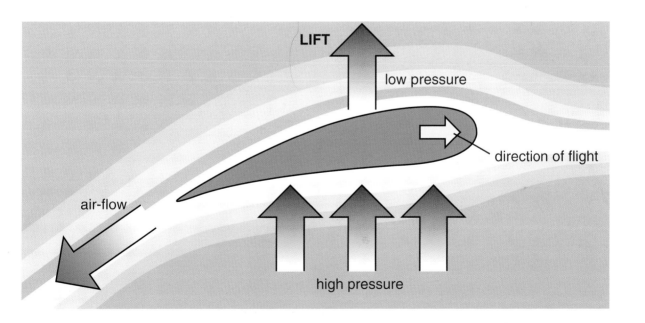

LIFT

low pressure

direction of flight

air-flow

high pressure

STRAIGHT UP

What do hot-air balloons, jump jets, helicopters and airships have in common? They can all hover or fly in one position above the Earth, without moving forwards or backwards. Hot-air balloons and airships float because they are lighter than air. Jump jets and helicopters, however, are heavier than air, so they have to keep 'pushing' to stay up. How can helicopters do this and why are balloons and airships lighter than air?

Floating

When you swim, you float. This is because the same volume of water as you weighs more than you do. This difference in weight gives you **buoyancy**, which was first explained by **Archimedes**. Hot-air balloons 'float' in the sky because hot air weighs less than the cold air that surrounds the balloon. In the past, airships were filled with hydrogen gas. It weighs much less than air, so the airships floated too.

DEW POWER?

Cyrano de Bergerac (1619–55), the French writer, noticed how morning dew rises off the ground in the heat of the sun's rays. In his writings, Cyrano suggested building an aircraft shaped like a huge glass ball, containing dew. When warmed by the sun, the dew inside would rise and take the aircraft with it. Cyrano proposed voyages to other planets, as well as flights on Earth.

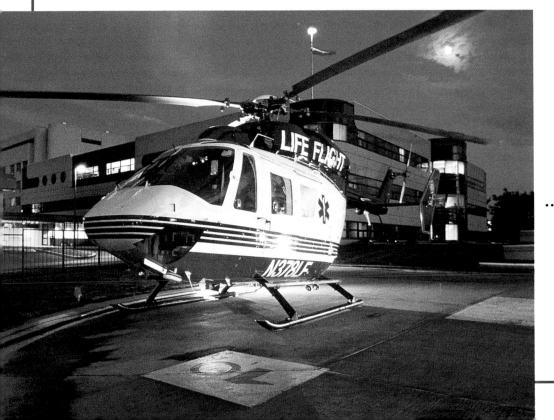

Helicopters are often used to rescue people in an emergency. They can take off and land in a small area.

Helicopters

Helicopters can fly straight up, forwards, backwards or hover in one place. The long, thin rotor blades lift the helicopter just as the wings of an aeroplane do. They also move it along. They are attached to a jet engine and, as the blades spin round, they pull the helicopter up into the air. The pilot changes the angle of the blades to change direction.

Balloons

The first hot-air balloon was made of paper and flew in 1753. A modern balloon is strong but light. It is made from nylon and coated with **polyurethane**. Hot air from a gas burner fills the balloon. Propane gas is stored as a liquid in cylinders inside the basket. The pilot controls the height by blasting hot air into the balloon.

Jump jets

Like a helicopter, a jump jet can take off from a small space, such as the deck of an aircraft carrier. The exhaust from the engine is directed downwards through four swivelling nozzles. This provides the lift. Once in the air, the nozzles swing back and the jump jet flies forwards like an ordinary fighter aircraft.

A balloon drifts above the countryside. The pilot controls the height by adjusting the burner.

The Hawker-Siddely Harrier jump jet does not need a runway to take off and land.

JET REVOLUTION

Most high-speed aircraft are driven by jet engines. So are helicopters, naval ships and even power stations that generate electricity. An experimental car has been designed with a jet engine, and one day we may even have our own jet packs for getting quickly from place to place. Just why are jet engines so popular and how do they work?

Jet engines are reliable and produce more power than most other engines of the same size. A jet engine of an aircraft is basically a tube which sucks in air at one end and uses it to burn fuel. It produces a stream of red-hot exhaust gases, which blasts backwards and thrusts the engine (and the aircraft) forwards. Jet engines get very hot so they are made of special, heat-resistant alloys to stop them melting. There are three main types of jet engine: the turbojet, the turboprop and the turbofan.

The turbojet

A turbojet has a turbine inside the engine. The turbine is spun by the stream of exhaust gases passing through it. The turbine compresses the air and pushes it through the engine more quickly.

Turbojets are noisy but small. Many warplanes use them because they can be easily fitted with afterburners to give them more power.

Turbojets are the simplest kind of jet engine. They work by pushing a jet of hot air out of the plane. This hits the air so fast that the reaction thrusts the plane forward, like a popped balloon.

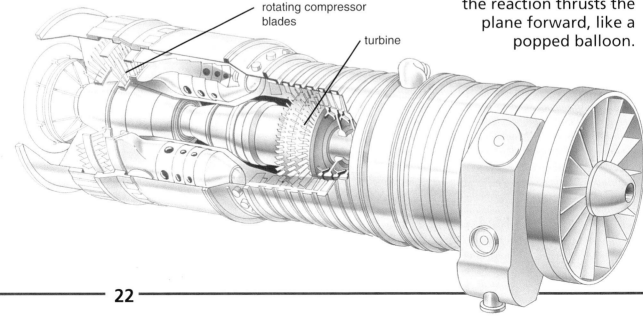

rotating compressor blades

turbine

The turboprop

The turbine in a turboprop engine is used to drive a propeller as well as a compressor. The propeller drives the plane forward. The hot exhaust gases also produce some thrust, as in a turbojet. Turbojets are slower than pure jets but they do not use so much fuel.

The turbofan

A turbofan engine has an enormous fan at the front that sucks in huge amounts of air. Most of the air bypasses the turbine and joins the exhaust gases, to give more thrust.

Turbofans are the best kind of jet engine for a passenger aircraft. They are quieter than turbojets and use less fuel. Nevertheless a jumbo jet may use 200,000 litres of fuel on a single flight from Europe to North America. The fuel is stored in large tanks in the aircraft's wings.

Although personal jet packs may seem an unlikely method of transport, and are currently used only by the army, maybe one day we will all use them to get around quickly!

NEWTON'S REACTION

Every action produces an equal but opposite reaction.

This is one of the famous laws of motion first stated by the English scientist, Sir Isaac Newton (1642–1727). According to this law, the forward motion of a jet aircraft is a result of reaction. The exhaust gases shooting back in the jet engine provide the action. The reaction is the thrust that propels the aircraft forwards.

SPACE TRAVEL

We have scarcely begun to explore the vast distances and billions of stars that make up the universe. For hundreds of years astronomers have studied the stars from Earth, but it was only 40 years ago that the first spacecraft was launched. Since then unpiloted probes have explored many of the planets, and today astronauts regularly shuttle backwards and forwards to space laboratories. How can space probes travel such huge distances and just what do astronauts do in space?

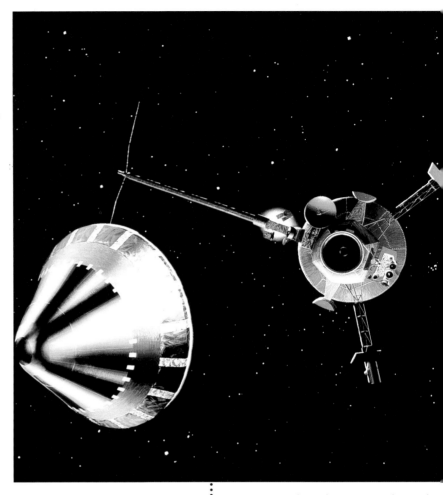

Slingshots in space

Since 1962 unpiloted probes have flown past every planet except Pluto. They are launched into space at the fantastic speed of 40,000 kilometres per hour (24,000 mph). They also use the pull of **gravity** of the planets they visit to boost their speed. First the gravity of the planet pulls them in, and they are accelerated by it. Then their speed becomes so great that they are flung out, with great force, into space, on a new course. Even so, their journey can take several years.

Probes need electricity to work their instruments. Those that explore the inner planets use solar power but those, such as *Galileo*, that travel to the outer planets use nuclear batteries instead.

Space probes have explored the solar system – the sun and the nine planets that orbit it. In 1995 *Galileo* travelled over 142,000 km (85,000 miles) to the planet Jupiter. The journey took five months. Here *Galileo* released a special probe to measure Jupiter's atmosphere. *Galileo* went on to explore Jupiter's many moons for two more years.

Hubble telescope

Probes send us photographs of the planets by radio, but to see beyond the planets to other stars and galaxies we have to rely on telescopes. Radio telescopes on Earth can pick up radio waves from stars billions of kilometres away, but the radio signals have to pass through the blanket of the Earth's atmosphere. In 1990 the Hubble telescope was launched into orbit around the Earth. It is now picking up and sending back much clearer information than telescopes on earth. For example, astronomers now have evidence of planets circling around other stars.

The Space Shuttle

The Hubble telescope could not have been launched without the help of the Space Shuttle. This re-usable spacecraft was first launched by the United States in 1981. It carries astronauts, satellites and equipment into orbit around the Earth. When the Hubble telescope was first launched, there was a fault with its main mirror. Astronauts on a later space-shuttle mission managed to repair the fault. Finally they succeeded and in 1994 the clearest pictures ever of deep space were beamed back to Earth.

The US space shuttle *Discovery* is rocketed into space.

LIGHT YEAR

A light year is a unit of length used in astronomy and space travel. A light year is equal to the distance that light travels in one year in a vacuum, or about 9.46 trillion km (5.88 trillion miles).

WHERE ARE WE?

Years ago, people explored the world using only compasses and other simple instruments to find their way. The magnet in a compass always points towards the Earth's magnetic north. Compasses on steel ships or aeroplanes can be affected by the metal of the ship and have to be specially protected. However, this protected type of compass does not work on a spacecraft. How can you find out where you are using a compass, and what do modern ships, aeroplanes and spacecraft use instead of magnetic compasses?

Triangulation

The magnetized needle in a compass always points north, towards the Earth's **magnetic pole**, so you can use it to find the direction, or bearing, of any object. If you find the bearing of two objects and draw them on a map, then your position is shown by the point where the lines cross.

Radio beacons

Ships and aircraft use radio beacons to calculate their exact position. This is the same method as triangulation with a compass, except that the bearings are calculated from the direction of the radio signals picked up by a receiver on the ship or aeroplane. The advantage of using radio signals is that they can be picked up at night or in fog.

This man wants to find out where he is. He is taking the bearings of two objects near him. If he then marks the bearings on a map, the point where the two lines meet wi!l be his position.

Gyrocompasses

Magnetic compasses are difficult to use on large ships because the needle is affected by steel and iron. A **gyroscope** is used instead. An electric motor is used to spin a wheel. Once the wheel is spinning its axis will always point in the same direction, like a spinning top while it spins fast. Spacecraft and space shuttles also use gyrocompasses to give them a fixed direction to steer by,

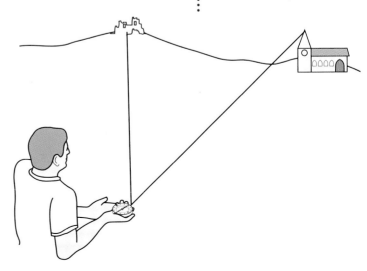

Steering by satellite

The Global Positioning System (GPS) uses 24 satellites orbiting in fixed positions above the Earth. The satellites send out radio signals which are picked up by special receivers on Earth. A computer inside the receiver then works out its exact position to within a few centimetres. Anyone can buy a special receiver and use GPS to find out where they are.

GPS was first designed for the US army, air force and navy. Now aircraft and ships use it too. In the future cars and other forms of transport will probably be fitted with receivers linked to GPS (see page 7). Already some bus companies, security firms and other organizations use GPS to tell them exactly where all their vehicles are. Each vehicle has a receiver fitted to the roof.

Convenient hand-held receivers allow hill-walkers to use the Global Positioning System.

INTO THE FUTURE

What will the future really hold? Will we travel about on jetpacks, as shown on page 23, or will there be an entirely new form of super-fast transport – such as teleporting, or energizing as in *Star Trek*? Entirely new technology is difficult to predict but one thing is certain: ordinary transport will have to cause less pollution. Maglev trains that use superconductors need very little electricity and give a smooth, fast ride. How do they work and what other sources of fuel might we be using in the future?

Magnetic trains

The smoothest trains have no wheels and are known as Maglev trains. 'Maglev' is short for magnetic levitation, a system which uses powerful **electromagnets** to lift the train a few centimetres above or below the track. Other magnets propel and guide the train. Experimental Maglev trains have already been developed in Germany and Japan, and at Birmingham in Britain a Maglev train carries people from the railway station to the airport.

This German overhead Maglev train uses very little electricity and creates less pollution than other trains.

Maglev trains do not have to overcome **friction** between the track and the train and so they can travel very fast. In Japan, one train carrying passengers reached a record 400.7 kilometres per hour (240.5 mph) along a seven-kilometre (4-mile) experimental track. In Germany the Maglev Transrapid has travelled at 412.6 kilometres per hour (247.5 mph).

Superconductors

Superconducting magnets could make Maglev transport very efficient. A superconductor loses all electrical resistance at very low temperatures, so electromagnets using it will need very little electricity. The race is on to find a material that superconducts at ordinary temperatures.

New fuels

Diesel and petrol are both made from oil, and one day oil supplies will run out. Manufacturers are looking for new sources of fuel. One possibility is vegetable oil, made from sunflower oil, or sugar. Already the Brazilians have made petrol from sugar cane which, unlike oil, can be replanted and will not run out. Burning fuel made from sugar or vegetable oil releases the carbon dioxide that was used when the plant grew (probably the year before). Burning fossil fuels release carbon dioxide that was trapped millions of years ago. Release of carbon dioxide into the atmosphere causes global warming.

A new fuel is being tested which is virtually pollution free. A fuel cell is a kind of battery that burns hydrogen to produce water and electricity. It was used first in spacecraft and in military vehicles, but soon it could be powering the cars on our streets. Fuel cells are almost 100 per cent efficient, which means they use almost all the energy obtained from burning hydrogen. This is much more efficient than petrol engines.

This bus in Vancouver, Canada, gets its energy from a fuel cell.

GLOSSARY

alloy a material that consists of two or more metals. This combination improves the properties of one of the metals.

Archimedes a famous ancient Greek mathematician, born about 287 BC. He founded the science of hydrostatics, which deals with floating objects.

buoyancy the upward thrust on an object that is immersed in a liquid. Archimedes discovered that the thrust is equal to the weight of the liquid displaced by the object.

compressor a machine or part of a machine which squashes air, increasing its pressure. Because the air in the combustion chamber of a jet engine is compressed, it expands very rapidly when the fuel burns, producing more thrust.

electromagnet a kind of magnet made of iron. It only becomes magnetic when an electric current flows in the coil of wire wrapped around it.

friction when two surfaces rub together, friction is the force that slows their movement and produces heat. Oil and grease are used to reduce the friction between the moving parts of an engine or the wheel-bearings on a vehicle.

gravity the force experienced by any object that has mass and is near to the Earth. It causes objects thrown in the air to fall back down to the ground. The force of gravity exists on other planets and moons, and depends on their mass and diameter.

gyroscope a spinning disc with a heavy rim. When it is set in any position, it resists any change of direction. As gyroscopes have this property they are used inside gyrocompasses.

hp (horsepower) this is used to measure the power of engines. It was originally used to compare the power of steam engines to the power of horses. In the metric system, engine power is measured in kilowatts (kW).

hydraulic hydraulics is the science of moving liquids through pipes. The hydraulic brakes of a vehicle work by transmitting forces through liquids in pipes.

internal combustion engine any engine in which the fuel is burned in combustion chambers inside the engine. Examples are petrol engines and diesel engines. In contrast, the fuel for a steam engine is burned in a separate furnace.

magnetic pole the region of a magnet from where its magnetic force appears to start. A bar magnet has a north pole at one end and a south pole at the other. The Earth has two magnetic poles.

nuclear reactor a nuclear reactor produces heat by splitting atoms of uranium in a controlled situation. The heat produced can be used to generate electricity.

polyurethane a kind of plastic

radar a system of sending radio waves in pulses. The reflections of these waves from a object are used to measure the object's distance and position.

satellite any small body that orbits around a much bigger one. The Moon is a natural satellite of the Earth; communications satellites for radio and television, and navigational satellites are artificial ones.

sensor a device that measures or senses conditions around it, such as temperature or pressure

solar power power obtained from the energy of the Sun's rays. The Sun gives us light and heat. The heat can be used directly. The light can be changed into electricity by solar panels.

solar system all the planets in orbit around the Sun. It also includes all the comets, asteroids and meteors.

streamlined a streamlined shape moves easily through a fluid, such as water or air. There is very little friction between the outside of the object and the fluid. The streamlined object offers little resistance, or drag.

superconductor a material that allows electricity to flow through it, at very low temperatures, without resistance (loss of energy). Ordinary conductors resist the flow of electricity.

FACT FILE

- The deepest dive ever made by a manned submersible took place on 23 January 1960. The bathyscaphe *Trieste* descended 10,916 metres into the Challenger Deep in the Pacific Ocean's Marianas Trench.

- The exploration of space began on 4 October 1957 when the first satellite, *Sputnik 1*, was launched by the Russians. Two years later, a Russian spacecraft took the first pictures of the far side of the Moon, which always faces away from Earth.

- The *Graf Zeppelin* (the first aircraft to circumnavigate the world) made over 500 transatlantic crossings. Between 1900 and 1939, 52,000 people travelled 2 million kilometres (1.2 million miles) by airship.

- The British *de Havilland Comet* was, in 1949, the first commercial jet airliner.

- Dick Rutan and Jeana Yeager flew non-stop around the world in 1986 in nine days. Their lightweight aircraft, *Voyager*, had twin engines and weighed 900 kilograms unladen. With all the fuel needed for its non-stop circumnavigation, it weighed 4210 kilograms.

- The first underground railway ran in London, between Farringdon and Edgeware Road, in 1863. It was 6.3 kilometres (3.9 miles) long, and used a steam locomotive.

INDEX